Mike Twohy

STOP, GO, YES, NO!

A STORY OF OPPOSITES

BALZER + BRAY
An Imprint of HarperCollinsPublishers

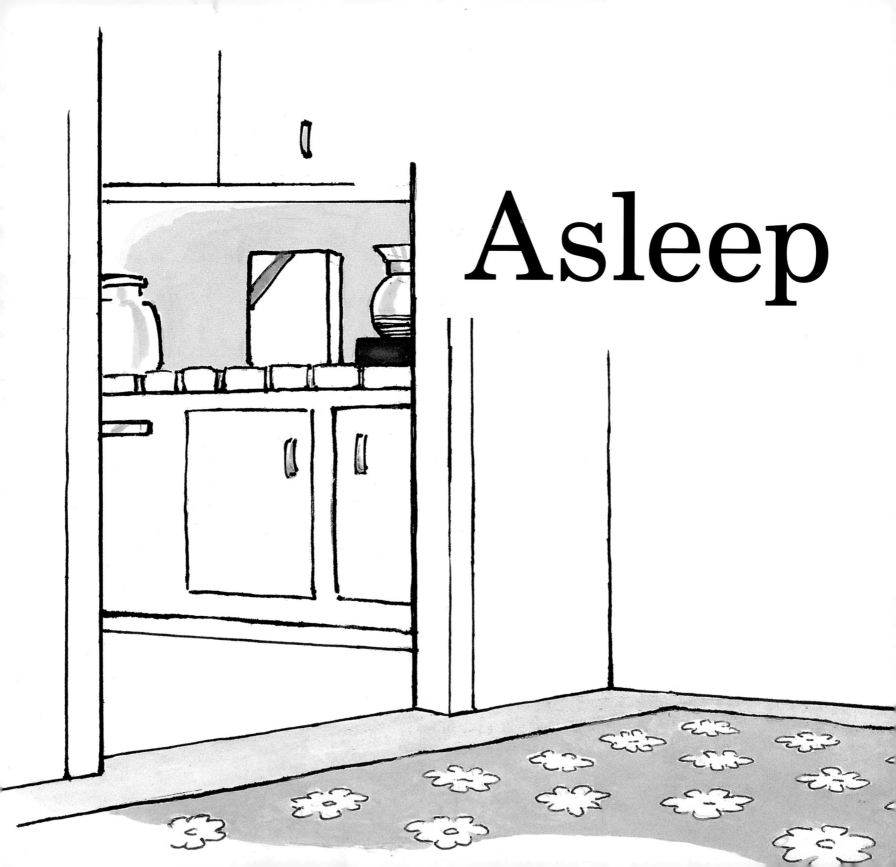

Awake

Over

Under

Smile

Frown

Wet

Dry

Hide

Seek

High

Low

Stop

Go

No!

Close

Far

Silly

Serious

Inside

Outside

Outside

Inside

Lost

Found

Apart

Together

For Linda, always

Balzer + Bray is an imprint of HarperCollins Publishers.

Stop, Go, Yes, No! A Story of Opposites
Copyright © 2018 by Mike Twohy

Library of Congress Control Number: 2017943278
ISBN 978-0-06-246933-5

The artist used India ink, felt-tip pens, and watercolor to create the illustrations for this book.
Typography by Dana Fritts and Laura Eckes
18 19 20 21 22 SCP 10 9 8 7 6 5 4 3 2 1

First Edition